In Tropics

by Penny Lee Forest

Harcourt
SCHOOL PUBLISHERS

Cover ©Photolibrary.com; 2 ©Photolibrary.com; 3 (l) ©Photolibrary.com; (r) ©Photolibrary.com; 4 (main) ©Photolibrary.com; (inset) ©Photolibrary.com; 5 ©Alamy; 6–7 ©Photolibrary.com; 8 (t) ©Photolibrary.com; (c) ©Alamy; (b) ©Alamy.

Printed in China

ISBN 10: 0-15-351321-7
ISBN 13: 978-0-15-351321-3

Ordering Options
ISBN 10: 0-15-351211-3 (Grade 1 Advanced Collection)
ISBN 13: 978-0-15-351211-7 (Grade 1 Advanced Collection)
ISBN 10: 0-15-358033-X (package of 5)
ISBN 13: 978-0-15-358033-8 (package of 5)

3 4 5 6 7 8 9 10   468   15 14 13 12 11 10 09 08

This place is in the tropics. Here, it is warm all year. There is also a lot of rain.

The tropics may be warm all year, but there are still four seasons. There are two wet seasons and two dry seasons.

In the wet seasons, there are big storms. The wind and water from the storms can move trees and rocks. The storms can make holes in houses!

There are many rain forests in the tropics. Some people live in the rain forest. These people live in huts. The huts are made from trees and leaves.

Some people live in houses on stilts. These houses are made from sticks and plants. When there is a lot of rain, the houses stay dry.

Some people in the tropics live in tall buildings. In the buildings, the air is cool.

People live in different ways in the tropics. They all need to stay cool and dry.